Carl Reynolds

Copyright © 2013 by Carl Reynolds

Hope—No Matter What
by Carl Reynolds

Printed in the United States of America

ISBN 9781628390681

All rights reserved solely by the author. The author guarantees all contents are original and do not infringe upon the legal rights of any other person or work. No part of this book may be reproduced in any form without the permission of the author. The views expressed in this book are not necessarily those of the publisher.

www.xulonpress.com

Contents

Introduction	vii
God is Real	9
What God Has Done For Us	11
What God Expects From Us	13
Listening to God	15
Talking to God	19
When (Not If) We Make Mistakes	21
Setting Priorities	23
What About Those With Different Beliefs?	27
Why Does God Allow Bad Things To Happen?	29
What is the Trinity?	31
Heaven and Hell	33
Summary	35
Thanks!	39

Introduction

What follows are some thoughts on God: why He is real; what He has done for us; what He expects from us; and why, no matter the situation, as long as we have a relationship with Him, there will always be **Hope–No Matter What**!

Carl Reynolds

God is Real

$\mathcal{B}$elief in anything that we can't see or that hasn't happened yet requires faith. For most of us, faith is not something that just automatically occurs or is all of a sudden magically there. It is based on things we experience and the inner feelings that develop from those experiences. We can't see the air we breathe, but know it's real because we've experienced the benefits. Since air has always been there for us, we have faith it will be available tomorrow and the next day and for the rest of our lives.

Belief in one Supreme Being who created everything is, especially in the beginning, difficult for many of us because we can't see Him and we don't understand Him. A personal relationship with our Creator first requires a personal belief in Him. So why should we believe to begin with?

Think about where each of us is at any moment in time—one human among around seven billion on the Earth, which is one of billions of planets, solar systems and galaxies in the universe. We are able to live, breathe, see, hear, smell, taste, feel, experience emotions, think and reason. To continue to exist, almost everything is dependent on almost everything else staying in perfect balance.

How did everything not only come into existence, but come into existence in perfect balance and stay in perfect balance for thousands of years? How could all of this have "just happened" as a result of some random chain of events? Something had to be in control, and has to still be in control. It has to have an intellect and powers far superior to those of any human. That something, I believe, is God.

Once we believe in and develop a relationship with Him, His hand in our lives begins to become more and more evident every day. Our faith that His Spirit is with us, through good times and bad, grows stronger and stronger, and finally, we believe more than any other thing that "He is real," and that long term we'll have **Hope—No Matter What!**

What God Has Done For Us

God created all things: the Universe, the Earth, Life, Us. He created Humans to live in union with Him, giving them not only a physical body, like the other living creatures, but a spiritual nature, as well. He is a Spiritual Being, and in ways, created us in his Own Spiritual Image.

Because we are created in His Spiritual Image—in order to live in union with Him—He is our Spiritual Father, and we can never experience true hope or have a clear direction in life unless we are living in a personal relationship with Him. This relationship comes from believing in Him and accepting His Word as the guideline for our lives.

What is His Word? God's Word "is" God. It represents His qualities, as well as the qualities He expects from those who live in a relationship with Him. He has shared His Word with Mankind throughout history in various ways—direct conversations, dreams, angels, prophets, etc.

Between 3,000 and 4,000 years ago, He gave the Word to Moses in writing—The Ten Commandments.

Around 2,000 years ago, He sent the Word to the world as a Human—Jesus Christ. Through Christ God did many things. Some include—

Teaching mankind more clearly the true meaning of His Word. (Its teachings had been seriously distorted by Humans after being given to Moses.)

Demonstrating, by example, how one's life should be lived in obedience to His Word. (He not only taught it, He lived it.)

Proving, as a result of Christ's sacrificial death and resurrection, that those who live in a relationship with Him will never die spiritually. For them, death is defeated—life lasts forever. No matter who they are, where they are or what they might be dealing with in their lives, God has given them **Hope—No Matter What!**

What God Expects From Us

*G*od expects us to live our lives in a personal relationship with Him. This relationship begins when we believe in His existence and accept His Word as the standard for our lives. It can begin anywhere, at any time. It is nurtured, made stronger and maintained much like other relationships in life — parents, children, friends, co-workers, etc. — by communicating with Him (talking and listening) often.

The primary ways we listen to God are by studying His Word and paying attention to those people around us who appear to be living their lives in a relationship with Him.

The primary ways we talk to God are prayer and serving our fellow man.

The more we communicate with Him, the stronger the relationship grows, the more faith we have that His Spirit is with us and the more sure we are that long term there is **Hope—No Matter What!**

Listening to God

*T*he Bible is God's Word in writing. When we read it, He is talking to us and expects us to listen. Some parts are much easier to understand than others. Some apply to us personally more than others. Some seem to contradict one another, while others most of us may never really understand.

However, even when confused we should remember the basic message is always the same —

There is one God who created us in His Own Image. He cares for us deeply and wants us to live in a relationship with Him. When we have that relationship, His Spirit is always with us, and once this Earthly Body dies our spirit will spend eternity in His Presence.

God also speaks with us through other people. These are not necessarily ministers, teachers or church congregational leaders. They are, many times, ordinary low-profile folks who live among us. Some of the characteristics most seem to have in common include—

> Their focus is almost always on others, not themselves. They willingly share their time and other resources with those who need help, and they don't boast about it. They know that "God knows," and that's what really counts. They've discovered that they themselves get as much or more out of serving others as those who they're helping get from them.

> They have the ability to "roll with life's punches." They are not immune to problems—health, financial, marital, family, etc. They are not perfect, making their share of mistakes. They do at times get "down," but usually get right back up and move on with their lives in a positive way.

> They are thankful for and satisfied with what they have, not covetous or jealous of others.

> They do not judge or gossip about others, understanding that God is the only Judge—the only Being with the ability to know a person's true motives—and that only He will ultimately decide who spends eternity with Him and who doesn't

> They rarely complain, realizing that success in this Earthly life is measured not in terms of

wealth, power, social status, popularity, etc., but rather in how well one plays the hand they're dealt. They know God's Spirit is with them, will sustain them, and long term there will be **Hope — No Matter What!**

Talking To God

The primary ways we talk to God are prayer and how we treat others.

When praying, we are talking to the most powerful Being in the universe — and He is listening. God does not care about the length of our prayer or how proper the wording is. He doesn't care if we whisper, yell, kneel, sit, stand up, bow our heads, look up, close our eyes or keep them open. He doesn't care who we are, where we're from or what we're wearing. He cares about what's in our hearts — our true motives — and the fact that we are taking the time to acknowledge Him and speak to Him.

Where "the rubber really hits the road" in our relationship with God is in how we treat others. We should remind ourselves often of what He has done, is doing and will do for us. Just as God cares for and helps us, we should, in turn, try to do the same for our neighbor.

Who is our neighbor? It's anyone we can help, beginning with those closest to us — family, friends, folks in the community, co-workers, etc. Sometimes we get so caught up in community events, civic organizations and even church congregational activities that we fail to put the proper priority on marriage, children, elderly parents or people living right around us who need help. I believe that one part of a right relationship with God involves asking Him to help us put our priorities in the right place at the right time.

When we put ourselves before others—and there are probably none of us who haven't been guilty of this at one time or another—we're missing the main point of what a true relationship with God is all about.

Whether we are praying or helping someone out, God is always there, He always listens and we know that long term we have **Hope—No Matter What!**

When (Not If) We Make Mistakes

Spiritually, in ways, we are created in the Image of God, and our spiritual inclination is to stay close to Him. However, because here on Earth we reside in this physical body, our Human inclination is to allow other things to come between God and us. When this happens, the result is sin—and we all sin. We make mistakes. It's not a matter of "if," but "when." God has provided a way that we can live our lives in a relationship with Him in spite of our mistakes. That "way" is found when, in our hearts, we believe in Him and accept His Word as the way we want to live.

It's like walking a road which represents life. At the end of that road is Heaven, and on each side there are ditches which represent sin. Our goal is to stay in the road until we reach its end. At times during the journey we wander off the path and fall into a ditch. If we have a right relationship with God, His Spirit will always be there to help us get out of the ditch and back onto the road toward an eternal presence with Him. We have **Hope—No Matter What!**

Hope–No Matter What

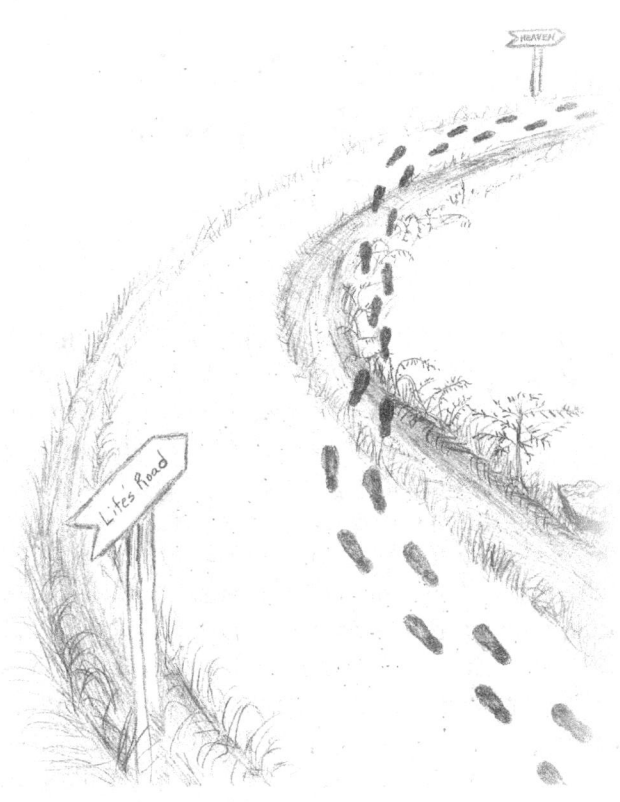

Setting Priorities

There are many opinions on setting priorities in life. One example—God first, family second, job third, etc. Another, for finances—first church, then family, debts, self, etc.

Many of us have struggled with this. How could anyone realistically give money to a church congregation first when they have kids at home who need food or clothes? What about a neighbor whose home has burned, or a family whose kid has cancer and no insurance?

Finally I have been able to resolve, for myself anyway, how this should work. We don't put the church congregation first—take care of our obligations there—then think to ourselves, "Well, that's done," and move on to the next item—i.e., check off One, then move on to Two, then Three, etc. Rather, we put our relationship with God at the center of everything and allow that relationship to constantly filter out and into every other part of life—family, neighbors, job, community, etc. God will then help us to deal wisely with the ranking of our priorities.

At different times along the way the rankings might vary depending on circumstances. But, if we do our best to keep a relationship with Him at the center of everything, He will always help us in our effort to do the right thing.

What About Those With Different Beliefs?

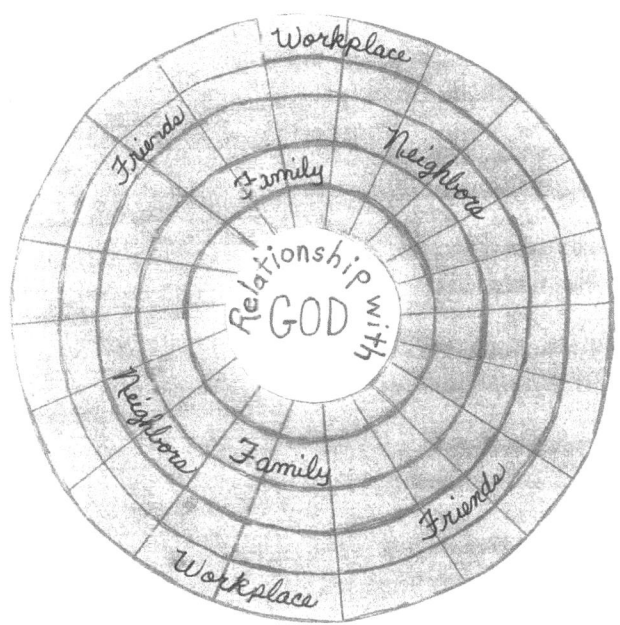

What About Those With Different Beliefs?

*T*here are roughly 7 billion people on Earth. Two billon practice Christianity—which includes thousands of different denominations. About 4 billion practice other religions, while around 1 billion practice no religion at all. Each of the 7 billion on the planet is a unique individual. None are perfect.

So, how does God expect us to relate to other folks who differ with us in their beliefs and practices? Does he want us condemning or pointing fingers at each other? No. God's Word tells us that He is the only Judge. He alone has the ability to look into the hearts of all people everywhere and understand their beliefs, their motives and why they are like they are. Bringing judgment on someone else's relationship with God is not what Christians (or anyone else) should be doing.

Does this mean that we shouldn't take a stand for our beliefs? No. Disagreeing or stating one's opinion is fine, but condemning or judging is not. Our focus should be on doing our best to "follow" the Word—which teaches to not pass judgment on others.

Doing our best to live according to the example set by Christ (the living Word) is much more likely to eventually advance the mission of Christianity than pointing fingers, chastising, gossiping, bickering or fighting over who is right and who is wrong.

God created all Humans the same. All are going to make mistakes. His wish—in spite of those mistakes—is for every person to believe in Him, accept His Word as a roadmap for living and spend eternity in His Presence. He wants "all" people everywhere to have **Hope—No Matter What!**

Why Does God Allow Bad Things To Happen?

*I*f there is an all-powerful God, why does He allow bad things to happen—especially to the innocent? Why the persecution of the early Christians, the Holocaust, slavery, starvation, disease, sexual abuse, murders, natural disasters, etc.?

Many have asked the question. My guess is that most everyone has thought it.

The truth is that no Human is any more capable of answering this than other age old questions, like, "Who made God?" or "How could one Being create the entire Universe?" or "How can God know the thoughts of everyone in the world simultaneously?"

I personally believe that, somehow, the bad things that happen to some people improve the chances of a far greater number of people being drawn into union with God and spending eternity in His Presence. But I sure don't understand "why" it has to work this way.

We just have to allow our faith to take over and believe that He is real and far superior to us in every way. We have to believe that He is in control and looking at things from a point of view that we are not capable of understanding; that this Earthly life is short term; that bad things will happen. But in spite of this, those who have a relationship with God will still have **Hope—No Matter What!**

What Is The Trinity?

According to Christian belief, *Trinity* is the term that refers to God as three Beings in one: the Father, Son and Holy Spirit—a difficult concept to understand. It's especially difficult to explain to children and others who are just being introduced to Christianity—not to mention those who are already skeptical.

To me, God is better described not as three Beings in one, but as one Being who has the ability to take different forms. He created us in His Own Spiritual Image to live in union with Him. He is our **Spiritual Father.**

He came to the world in the form of a human (Jesus Christ) to teach and demonstrate by example what a relationship with God means. He then proved, as a result of Christ's sacrificial death and resurrection, that those who live their lives in a relationship with Him will, in spite of their Earthly transgressions, be united with Him for eternity. This human form of God (Jesus Christ) is the **Son.**

God is a Spiritual Being and has the ability to be with every person—everywhere, all the time—and will help those who have a relationship with Him to deal with whatever situation they may face. This form of God is the **Holy Spirit.**

In dealing with Biblical concepts like the Creation, the Resurrection, the Trinity, etc., we again have to fall back on our belief in the one God, who has powers far beyond our Human ability to comprehend. He created all things, including us. He wants us to live our lives in a relationship with Him by accepting His Word, which in human form was Jesus Christ. If we have that relationship, His spirit is with us and we have **Hope—No Matter What!**

Heaven and Hell

*T*he Bible speaks of Heaven as having "streets paved with gold," and of Hell as being a "lake of fire." Are these terms literal or symbolic? I don't know, but my guess is that Heaven is probably a lot better than "streets paved with gold," and Hell is much worse than a "lake of fire."

What God's Word is pretty clear on is—

> Those who, in this Earthly life, neither believe in God nor accept His Word will eventually die physically. Their spirits will then be forever separated from Him, with no hope of reconciliation. This is **Hell.**

> Those who, in this Earthly life, believe in God and accept His Word as the guideline for their lives will also, at some point, die physically. However, their spirits will go on to be in His presence forever. This is **Heaven**, and why

those who are living in a relationship with Him always have **Hope—No Matter What!**

Summary

God is real and made all things—including life. He is a Spiritual Being, creating Humans in his Own Spiritual Image. He is our Spiritual Father.

God cares for us deeply and wants everyone to live in a relationship with Him forever.

We, as Humans, can never experience true hope, or have a clear direction in life, unless we have that relationship.

We find a relationship with God by believing in Him and accepting His Word as the standard for our lives.

God's Word has existed since the beginning. It represents not only His qualities, but the qualities he expects from those living in a relationship with Him.

Since the beginning, He has shared the Word with Mankind in many ways—angels, prophets, dreams, the Ten Commandments, etc.

Two thousand years ago, God sent his Word to the world as a Human—Jesus Christ. While on Earth, Christ taught and demonstrated by example the true meaning of a relationship with God.

God then proved, as a result of Christ's sacrificial death and resurrection, that those who do live in a relationship with Him will never die spiritually, but spend eternity in His Presence. For them, death is defeated—life goes on forever.

The Holy Spirit is that form of God that has the ability to be with every person, everywhere, all the time—and to give hope and comfort to those who have a relationship with Him no matter what their situation.

It is important for us to communicate with God often—reading the bible, praying, helping others, etc.

We will make mistakes because we are Human. We should remember, however, that God's Spirit is always with us and is not only aware of "what" we do, but our "motives" for doing what we do—and He forgives. He will help us to "get out of the ditch" and on with our lives in a relationship with Him.

God is the only judge of who has a relationship with Him and who doesn't. He alone has the ability to look into the hearts of all people everywhere and understand their beliefs, their motives and why they are like they are.

Those who, in this Earthly life, neither believe in God nor accept His Word as their way of living will eventually die physically. Their spirits will then be forever separated from Him with no hope of reconciliation. This is Hell.

Those who, in this Earthly life, believe in God and make the right effort, in their hearts, to follow his Word will also, at some point, die physically.

Summary

However, their spirits will go on to be in His Presence forever. This is Heaven, and why those who are living their Earthly lives in a relationship with Him always have **Hope—No Matter What!**

Thanks!

Thanks to my wife for her input, illustrations and the last 42 years.

Thanks to our children for asking so many questions while growing up.

Thanks to the grandchildren who are now asking more questions.

More than anything thanks to God for **Hope — No Matter What!**

About the Author

Carl Reynolds is the author of three previous children's books: *Why Frogs Have No Hair, The Turkey Mountain Gang—The Adventures Begin* and *The Turkey Mountain Gang's Christmas Adventure*. He and his wife, Kathy, live in rural Virginia. They've been married for 42 years, have two children and 4 grandchildren. Carl grew up on a farm, attended Virginia Tech, served in the military and is retired from VF Corporation.

www.ingramcontent.com/pod-product-compliance
Lightning Source LLC
LaVergne TN
LVHW021742060526
838200LV00052B/3431